Bux

Guide &

Lindsey Porter

A E

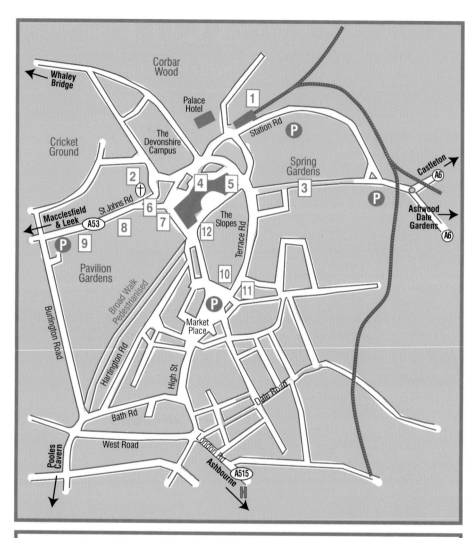

BUXTON

"Gateway to the Peak District..."

Buxton is a lovely Georgian spa town that stands on the edge of the Peak District. As you drop down into the town from the high heather moors, you enter a world of almost forgotten elegance.

The Crescent

Buxton has played host to visitors since the Romans discovered the quality of its warm spa water and established a settlement here. From the Middle Ages, its healing qualities brought more people in the hope of a cure from their ailments. Amongst these was Mary, Queen of Scots who came with her erstwhile gaoler, William, 6th Earl of Shrewsbury, to seek the benefits of the spa and no doubt a change of scenery and air as well. The Earl was the fourth husband of Elizabeth, Bess of Hardwick, and founder of the Cavendish dynasty.

The Cavendish family have maintained that link with the town, which has benefited greatly by it. Today, the area of Buxton most associated with the heritage of the town consists of buildings and public open space created by different Dukes of Devonshire, the head of the Cavendish family.

The town remains as popular as ever with visitors. The highest town in the country means that spring comes later here, but its tourists seldom seem to mind. A £3 million pound investment in the restoration of the Pavilion Gardens is one of the most recent in a list of developments designed to improve facilities for visitors who come from all over the world to see its sights and enjoy its impressive Festivals.

So welcome to Buxton, where old and new blend well together, we extend a welcome to both new visitors as well as our regular friends.

A hundred years ago, there would be many residents who could look back and remember when Buxton was essentially a village. It was an elegant one too, with visitors who came to the spa, famous for its healing properties from the warm thermal waters of its spring.

Old guidebooks tell you that the original hall has been demolished, but how wrong they were! Recent detective work has revealed that the original four-storey hall of the Elizabethan period does, in fact, still survive. It may be seen from Hall Bank or from the adjacent lawned area known as The Slopes. Looking at the side of the Old Hall Hotel, two bay windows rise the full height of the building. This section is the old hall. Although chiefly refaced with stone and extended to the left and right, a little of the original external stonework survives to the left of the left hand bay, including the join where the extension of 1670 butted up to the original masonry. It is the oldest building in the town, dating from 1572.

Inside this pleasant hotel, a large room on the first floor of the old hall, which would have originally faced the sun, was the principal bedroom. It is called the Scots Room to this day, recalling the five visits between 1573 and 1584 of Mary, Queen of Scots. The original garden of the hall extended to the thermal spring and also across The Square where the former Hall Garden is now incorporated within the Pavilion Gardens.

Proceeding towards the Crescent, on the right are The Slopes. This area was used as a place of exercise by those taking "the Cure", the aim being to be able to forsake the Buxton Basket-chair and eventually walk to the top. Many of the large stone

Right: The Old Hall Hotel

Below: The Scots Room

urns remain, creating a pleasant air of elegance often missing in municipal gardens. The Slopes were not laid out until 1818 by Sir Jeffrey Wyatville but were remodelled by Joseph Paxton in about 1840. The garden was originally known as St Anne's Cliff and the urns date from 1818.

Next to the Old Hall Hotel is the former Town Baths, opened on May 17th 1924, after being remodelled. This was later transferred to the Pavilion Gardens in 1972. It had been originally built as the Natural Baths in 1853 on the site of the ancient spring used by the Scottish Queen Mary, along with other aristocrats including The Earls of Essex and Leicester, and had a glass-roofed passage connecting it to the Hall Hotel. The original St Anne's drinking well was situated on the corner of the building where it met The Crescent. The separate entrances to the mens' and ladies' natural baths were next to it, off the colonnade which goes down the back of The Crescent, between this building and the Baths. The latter had been built by Henry Currey and he was responsible for several other buildings in the town.

Today the Natural Baths are being converted to a new Thermal Spa Hotel as part of a Crescent Spa restoration programme, costing £32m.

Opposite this building is the current St Anne's Well at the foot of The Slopes. It must be one of the most frequented wells surviving in this country and it is likely to remain so. Here you can fill up your bottles with a free supply of mineral water. It is warm, too, having a temperature of 27.5^0 C (about 80^0 F).

St Anne's Drinking Well

The provision of this water supply for the village, together with the well in the Market Place, in 1840, was a boon to inhabitants, especially those from Upper Buxton who no longer had to trudge up the hill with their water. It was celebrated then by dressing the wells and the event became a tradition, which has continued to this day.

Adjacent to the Well is The Pump Room. This was built in 1894 and was a popular venue for visitors who wished to drink the water, which bubbled up into a white marble lined well. This was converted into a Micrarium in 1981, which has now closed, and is currently used by the Pump Room Artists. It was designed by Henry

Currey and originally had domes on each end. It was also colonnaded, like the Crescent, but these have now been infilled to make the interior larger.

Opposite the Pump Room is the Crescent. Built between 1780 and 1790 (although part was in use from 1786), it was the first important imitation of the Crescent at Bath. Here, however, the design was much smaller and compact. It was designed by John Carr of York. It has a very distinctive colonnade; it is semi-circular in shape and has 378 windows! Prior to its construction, a major complaint about the then small village of Buxton was that there was a dire shortage of accommodation. The building was built with this in mind and was used as three hotels. St Anne's Hotel was at the west or left-hand side, The Centre Hotel (not suprisingly) was in the middle and the Great at the right-hand side. The building was financed by the Duke's profit from the Ecton Copper Mine in the Manifold Valley. Pevsner's *Buildings of England* quotes the cost as being £38,600. In 1781, the sale of ore from the mine, for this one year alone, realised nearly £45,000, a huge amount of money at the time. Today the building is empty, but not for long. It is being refurbished and we should soon see it in use again, after a £32m programme.

To the right of the Crescent were the Hot or Thermal Baths. These have been converted to a rather pleasant arcade of shops. Much of the Minton tiling survives together with a plunge bath and seat, which lowered people down into the water. The original roof was created in the ridge and furrow pattern, used by Paxton on the Chatsworth Greenhouse and then the Crystal Palace. An attractive stained glass roof has now replaced this. Currey built the Baths in 1854 and the conversion to shops was in 1987. It was a creative scheme and a good use for the redundant baths.

Behind The Crescent and standing in large grounds is the former Devonshire Royal Hospital, now The Derby University. This was originally the stable for The Crescent and was built with a circular, colonnaded courtyard for exercising the horses. It was built in 1785-90 as a second phase to

Above: The Pump Room Right: Artistic detail from the Pump Room Opposite page: The Crescent, lamp standard and urn of 1818 brought from Lismore, Ireland

The Crescent. It originally had stabling for 300 horses and accommodation for the coachmen and grooms. In 1859, it was converted to a hospital for "the use of the sick poor". The scheme was not without opposition; Paxton was worried about the occupants descending on the Hall Gardens, for instance. The reason the building has so much ground around it was to provide an exercise area for the sick. The hospital was financially supported by the Buxton Baths Charity and although it afforded relief for sufferers of rheumatism and related illnesses, the occupants had their own bath and exercise area. They were not encouraged to mingle with guests paying good money to take the waters!

In 1881-82, in a bold and imaginative scheme, the courtyard was given a dome. At the time, it was the largest unsupported dome in the world and it still ranks as one of the largest. It weighs 560 tons. The acoustics are good too; standing in the middle of the dome underneath the lantern, you have to be careful of what you say, for everyone can hear you. For years, this splendid building had been one of the few NHS hospitals that welcomed visitors, as well as patients to the building, and even sold a guidebook.

With its Tuscan columns arranged in a circular pattern, the interior is very impressive.

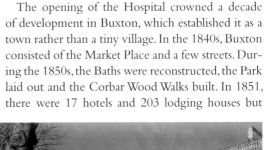

The opening of the Hospital crowned a decade of development in Buxton, which established it as a town rather than a tiny village. In the 1840s, Buxton consisted of the Market Place and a few streets. During the 1850s, the Baths were reconstructed, the Park laid out and the Corbar Wood Walks built. In 1851, there were 17 hotels and 203 lodging houses but

Above and Right: Devonshire Dome

Bottom: The old "Buxton Baths" sign

still no provision for non-conformist religion except for the Methodist Church which opened in the Market Place two years previously. It was 1861 before the Roman Catholic Church opened in Terrace Road. Until then, the priest had come over the moors from Leek. The Congregational Church (designed by Currey) had opened in 1859. St Anne's Church, the original village church, had been re-opened for religious use again in 1842. The Market Place also saw the erection of a Market Hall in 1857, but it burnt down in 1885. By the 1860s Buxton was maturing as a town community and came of age with the arrival of the railway.

Across Manchester Road, which runs up the left hand side of the former Devonshire Hospital, is the Church of St John the Baptist. This was built in 1811 and stands on 2,200 piles, each 16 feet long. It was built after some criticism that the town put a greater emphasis on revelry rather than religion. The village did have St Anne's Church in Higher Buxton, but it was out of the way, being just off the far end of the High Street. In fact, had it been in Lower Buxton, it is likely that it would have been demolished to make way for a more imposing structure. To that extent, it's just as well it was situated out of the way!

The building of 1811 is described by Pevsner as more Italian than Classical, with its Tuscan columns and pilasters, and a tower with a dome unique for that period. Its elegant design was very much in keeping with the lower town in the early years of the 19th Century.

The 1850s was a defining moment in the development of the village into a town and in the few years which followed this was to be developed further. The railway reached Buxton in 1863 and marked the beginning of a new era for the new town. At the start of that decade, the population was a little over 4,000, but this had gone up by over 1,000 by 1871. The railway had a pronounced effect on tourism too. It must have come as a shock to find that for the well dressing ceremony, a few days after the opening of the railway, some 20-30,000 visitors came to the town. The railway, of course, brought even more visitors throughout the year.

Next to and looking down onto the railway and The Crescent, is the Palace Hotel. It was built in 1867-68, to the design of Henry Currey. It was the first major development after the railway but was soon to be followed by the Pavilion, its Concert Hall and the Gardens.

At the town end of the Pavilion lies the Opera House which has a loyal following and plays an important part of the annual Buxton Festival and the Gilbert and Sullivan Festival, although its doors are open all year round with a wide variety of entertainment. It was built in 1903 by Frank Matcham and has a splendidly restored interior. It is well respected for the quality of its performances and the town is fortunate to have it.

To the left of the entrance to the Opera House is the Conservatory. Other than being nice and warm on a cold day, it is well-stocked with flowering plants and unusual trees and shrubs. It really shouldn't be missed and is popular with visitors and locals alike. At the upper end, is the Pavilion, built in 1871. Around 1981, this building was needlessly set on fire by an arsonist. During its restoration, the opportunity was taken to incorporate another floor, that now houses a Coffee Shop. It has lovely views out into the Pavilion Gardens and the more curious can discover how the weight of the floor was carried on the existing cast-iron columns. If you are lucky, you may be serenaded from the recently built bandstand outside.

Adjacent is the Concert Hall, added five years later in 1876. There is a continual programme of events here, including antique and classic car sales. Virtually a hundred years later, the swimming pool was built next to the Concert Hall. It has the bonus of using the warm thermal spa water. It's not often that a municipal authority can exercise the largesse of filling its baths with mineral water. Next to the swimming pool is one of the town's carparks, built on the site of the former curling rink.

A pleasant recent addition to the Pavilion Gardens has been the Band Stand. There

Palace Hotel

used to be one directly in front of The Pavilion but on the far side of the River Wye, that flows through the Gardens. The new one is fairly close to The Pavilion and on the near side of the river. The old one was used for concerts on a daily basis in the summer, with three concerts a day. Once more the Band Stand will be used for concerts every summer, together with special celebrations.

The Gardens were originally laid out as the Serpentine Walks, but when these were remodelled into their present design, part of the original was left alone. Along with Corbar Woods, it must be one of the town's best kept secrets. To find it, leave the Gardens at Burlington Road and walk along St John's Road. Virtually opposite Park Street is a path to the left that leads down to the River Wye. Take this or continue along the road until you have just crossed the river and then take the path. Both bring you back to Burlington Road at the side of the Pavilion Gardens.

Below the Opera House is The Square, which is the name of the street as well as the colonnaded building on the side opposite the Pavilion Gardens. Above is the Old Club House, now a pub, with the Opera House, the Conservatory and the entrance to the Pavilion Gardens opposite. The colonnaded Square was built in 1802-03. It was originally fashionable accommodation. Opposite the Opera House, and between the Square and The Old Club House, is a letter box bearing the monogram VR. It was erected in 1867 and is the only one of its kind in the county. The Old Club House

The Pavillion and gardens

The Opera House

Left and Above: The Bandstand and gardens

The Opera House

used to be the Union Club and you had to be a member to drink there. Now it offers a wider welcome and is popular with theatre-goers. It has a unique atmosphere and its worth looking through the windows even if you don't wish to enjoy the hospitality. Next to The colonnades of The Square is The Old Hall Hotel, The Slopes and Hall Bank which takes you up to the Market Place and Town Hall.

Across the road from the latter is the town's Museum and Art Gallery on The Terrace. Formerly the Peak Hydropathic and Hotel (sic), it has a lot to interest any visitor. This is an excellent museum for a small town and houses ornaments in Blue John stone from Castleton and inlaid black marble from Ashford-in-the-Water. The finds from several caves in the Manifold Valley are kept here and the study of Sir William Boyd Dawkins has been recreated. It is fascinating to compare the Victorian study with its modern equivalent. The Museum looks down towards Spring Gardens, the main shopping street of the town that now incorporates a modern undercover development with several national High Street shops.

The town is not only a good shopping centre, it is also a good centre for exploring the Peak District too. Buxton has changed its role over the centuries, from a village community to its heyday as a notable spa town. It still serves the visitor well and is clearly determined to ensure that it continues to do so. With an eye to conservation and maintaining all that is good in the town, it entertains and serves visitors and locals alike with its Festival; performances at the Opera House from ballet to brass bands; its shopping facilities and its pivotal role as a gateway to the Peak District.

A stroll around Buxton

From the Crescent cross the road to the Grove Hotel, with the Victorian glass-roofed veranda extending along the street. Turn left and then right and take Station Approach to reach the Railway Station. The new road cuts across the former Midland Railway Station. It was identical to the L&NWR Station of which the end wall survives

The Town Hall

with its fan-shaped window. Trains still run to Manchester's Piccadilly Station.

Continue on down George Street. On the left is the former bath for residents of the hospital plus the Old Court House, now redeveloped with shops and restaurants. The former George Hotel on the right is now apartments. Ahead is The Square.

On the north side of St John's Road, in the middle of the Park, is the Cricket Ground. County matches are no longer held here, however Buxton made national headlines in the mid 1970's when snow stopped play in June!

Once you are ready to leave the Gardens, proceed to the southern end, where Burlington Road meets Broad Walk, the pedestrianised roadway on the east side of the Gardens. Turn left here up Bath Street. The name is a reminder of the former swimming baths that used to exist on the corner of Macclesfield Road and Burlington Road. At the top of Bath Street, on the right, is the old church dedicated to St Anne. It was built in 1625 and is believed to be the second oldest property in the town. It looks too secular to be a church and in fact was used as a school after the new church was opened. With its low roof and exposed wooden tie beams, it is easy to imagine it being used for a secular purpose. It has no tower or aisles and is an unusual survivor.

At the end of Bath Street is High Street, which leads into the Market Place. This is a busy place on Tuesdays and Saturdays when the market traders stalls are erected. The area is dominated by the Town Hall, built in 1887. The old Market Cross survives on its plinth in the middle of the Market Place, but like many other towns, the main use of the wide open space is for carparking. This area will soon be re-developed to create a friendlier pedestrian area. The cross is thought to be 15th Century, but as the town has only had a market charter since 1813, this cross celebrates that event. It was previously situated near to The Palace Hotel. Notice the Eagle Hotel on the left. It was built by the Duke of Devonshire as a hotel in 1760. The Duke held most of the rights to the turnpike roads in the Peak and built quite a few hotels as a result. One of the better known of these is the Snake Inn on the Snake Pass, on the A57 east of Glossop.

The Town Hall originally had a small museum, but this grew too big and a fresh site was provided on the Terrace in 1928.

Interior of of Hargreaves China Shop

Left: Spring Gardens Shopping Centre
Right: The Victorian pillar box, near the Opera House

From here, one soon descends down to Spring Gardens, with its covered Shopping Centre and some national high street names. At least Buxton has more public open space than most towns and Spring Gardens has also been pedestrianised.

Buxton may no longer be a fashionable spa town where one came to see and be seen. The Bath Chairs have long gone and its water no longer brings relief to thousands of rheumatoid patients a year. The name "Buxton Water" is perhaps better known across the country because of the plastic mineral bottles that bear the name. Nonetheless, Buxton has adapted to the short-break and conference market as well as the day visitors; longer stay visitors remain for the Buxton Festival which is a credit to the town, complimenting the magnificently refurbished Opera House that offers a choice of opera, comedy, drama, dance, ballet and music. The town has much to offer; welcome to Buxton.

ATTRACTIONS

Buxton Museum & Gallery

Terrace Road, Buxton SK17 6DA
☎ 01298 24658
Email: buxton.museum@derbyshire.gov.uk
Open: Tues–Fri 9.30am–5.30pm; Sat 9.30am–5pm; Sun & BH (Easter to end-Sep 10.30am–5pm). Free Admission. Regularly holds exhibitions of paintings, photography and ceramics.

Buxton Opera House

Water Street, Buxton SK17 6XN
Box Office: ☎ 0845 127 2190
Enquiries: admin@boh.org.uk
www.buxtonoperahouse.org.uk
Varied programme see above for information.

Pavilion Gardens

St John's Road, Buxton SK17 6XN
☎ 01298 23114
Email: paviliongardens@highpeak.gov.uk
www.paviliongardens.co.uk
Over 23 acres of gardens including lakes, flower beds, children's play area and a miniature railway. In the pavilion is a food and gift shop, restaurant, café, concert hall, conservatory and conference centre. Fairs and events are held throughout the year.

Poole's Cavern & Country Park

Green Lane, Buxton
☎ 01298 26978
www.poolescavern.co.uk
Open: February, weekends 10am-4pm; March onwards daily, 9.30am-5pm
Pooles Cavern is a natural limestone cave formed over millions of years and situated in the beautiful woodland of Buxton Country Park. Guided tours of the cavern last approximately 50 minutes and leave every 20 minutes throughout the day. Expert guides will lead you through illuminated chambers and passages to the final chamber 300m (1,000ft) from the entrance.

A 20-minute brisk walk from Poole's Cavern takes you to the summit of Grin Hill. Here is Buxton's very own folly, Solomon's Temple, built in 1896. From here on a clear day you can see as far as 24km (15m).

Buxton Festival

ENTERTAINMENT

Buxton is well known for music and the arts. Its festival in the summer holds numerous artistic events including its opera programme, Literary Festival, the International Gilbert & Sullivan Festival and 'The biggest Fringe Festival in England' with hundreds of performances from Comedy to Drama, Music to Film, Visual Arts to the Spoken Word.

The Opera House also has a varied programme of drama, opera, ballet, dance, music, children's shows and traditional pantomime.

ACCOMMODATION

Lists of various types of accommodation may be obtained from the Tourist Information Centre. There is a full range of serviced accommodation: hotels, guest houses, bed & breakfast, farm houses, youth hostels, camp and caravan sites.

TOURIST INFORMATION CENTRE

Pavilion Gardens, St Johns Road, Buxton SK17 6XN

☎ 01298 25106 Email: tourism@highpeak.gov.uk

www.visitpeakdistrict.com

OTHER INFORMATION

Banks: there are several banks, all with cash machines. Most are in Spring Gardens or around the corner in The Quadrant.

Cricket: The Park

Golf Courses: Cavendish ☎ 01298 79708; Buxton & High Peak ☎ 01298 26263

Market Days: Tuesday & Saturday. Farmer's Market in The Pavilion, 1st Thursday of month 10am-3pm.

Swimming Pool: Pavilion Gardens ☎ 01298 766142

Tennis & Bowls: Ashwood Park (far end of Spring Gardens)

Toilets: Car park, far end of Spring Gardens; Market Place; and Pavilion Gardens

---

Ashbourne Editions, The Oaks, Moor Farm Road West, Ashbourne, DE6 1HD
Tel: O1335 347349 Fax: 01335 347303

3rd edition

ISBN: 978-1-873775-25-7
© Lindsey Porter 2010

Design & cartography: Michelle Prost
Printed by: Gutenberg Press, Malta

Photography by:
Buxton Festival (www.buxtonfestival.co.uk): Front cover, p.12 top & bottom Left, p.15
Visit Peak (www.visitpeakdistrict.com): Back cover top middle & top right, p.8 top & middle, p.10 top & bottom left, p.11 bottom right, p.12 right,
Mark Titterton: Back cover middle, p.4 right, p.10 right, p.11 top
All other photography: Lindsey Porter & Hedley Alcock

Front cover: Opera House exterior at dusk
Back cover: Top Left: Band Stand in Pavilion Gardens, **Top Middle:** Opera House, **Top Right:** Opposite 'The Slopes', **Bottom:** Pavilion Gardens